First World War
and Army of Occupation
War Diary
France, Belgium and Germany

34 DIVISION
Divisional Troops
176 Brigade Royal Field Artillery
28 May 1915 - 28 August 1916

WO95/2448/2

The Naval & Military Press Ltd
www.nmarchive.com
Published in association with The National Archives

Published by

The Naval & Military Press Ltd

Unit 10 Ridgewood Industrial Park,

Uckfield, East Sussex,

TN22 5QE England

Tel: +44 (0) 1825 749494

www.naval-military-press.com

www.nmarchive.com

This diary has been reprinted in facsimile from the original. Any imperfections are inevitably reproduced and the quality may fall short of modern type and cartographic standards.

© Crown Copyright
Images reproduced by permission of The National Archives, London, England, 2015.

Contents

Document type	Place/Title	Date From	Date To
Heading	34th Division 176th Brigade R.F.A. Jan-Aug 1916 Broken Up.		
Miscellaneous	176th (Leicester) RFA Houritzer Brigade		
Heading	176th Brigade R.F.A. Vol II 34		
War Diary	Leicester	28/05/1915	30/08/1915
War Diary	Tidworth Park	30/08/1915	02/10/1915
War Diary	Boyton Camp	04/10/1915	22/10/1915
War Diary	Boyton	03/11/1915	16/12/1915
Heading	176th Bde. R.F.A. Vol I TA IV Jan 16 Aug 16		
War Diary	Boyton	20/12/1915	08/01/1916
War Diary	Le Havre	09/01/1916	09/01/1916
War Diary	Inghem	11/01/1916	21/01/1916
War Diary	Blaringhem	21/01/1916	18/02/1916
War Diary	Armentieres	19/02/1916	29/02/1916
Heading	176 RFA Vol 3		
War Diary	Armentieres	01/03/1916	23/04/1916
War Diary	Armentieres	01/04/1916	22/04/1916
War Diary	Armentieres	22/04/1916	23/04/1916
War Diary	Quelmes	24/03/1916	29/03/1916
War Diary	Albert	16/05/1916	31/05/1916
War Diary	Albert	30/05/1916	30/05/1916
War Diary	Albert	01/06/1916	30/06/1916
Miscellaneous	For Use In The Field. Account of sums received and expended by the Sub-Accountant during the month of April 1916 in account With the.		
Miscellaneous	HQ 176 Inf Bde.	30/04/1916	30/04/1916
Miscellaneous			
Miscellaneous		16/04/1916	16/04/1916
Miscellaneous		25/04/1916	25/04/1916
Miscellaneous	AG's Officer 3rd Echelon.	02/06/1916	02/06/1916
Miscellaneous	25 April 1916 Been Power 75 Kilos Pournies by taken a 72.7.G	25/04/1916	25/04/1916
Heading	34th Div. III. Corps. War Diary Headquarters 176th Brigade R.F.A. July 1916		
War Diary	Albert	01/07/1916	31/07/1916
Heading	34th Divisional Artillery. 176th Brigade Royal Field Artillery August 1916		
War Diary	Albert	01/08/1916	17/08/1916
War Diary	Eontalmaison.	18/08/1916	24/08/1916
War Diary	Armentieres	25/08/1916	28/08/1916
Miscellaneous	176 F.A. Bde.		

34TH DIVISION

175TH BRIGADE R.F.A.
JAN - AUG 1916.

BROKEN UP

176th (Leicester) RFA Howitzer Brigade

A short history of the raising of the above Brigade.

Towards the end of May 1915 an enquiry was forwarded by Major Meysey Thompson M.P. to the Leicester Recruiting Committee with regards to forming a Howitzer Brigade in Leicester. The Committee having decided that this should be done, the following local gentlemen were appointed for the purpose of carrying it out —

Presidents — His Grace. The Duke of Rutland
His Worship. The Mayor of Leicester. (Alderman J North J.P.)

Chairman — His Worship. The Mayor of Leicester.
Vice Chairman — Sir Samuel Faire J.P.
Committee — Evan Barlow Esq, Councillor Collier, H Flude Esq, T E Meakin Esq, Major H W Plant.

Hon Brigade Accounting Officer — W Penn Lewis Esq (Boro Treasurer)

Hon Organizing Secretary — J. H. Crumbie Esq.

Major Meysey Thompson was officially the Raiser of the Brigade.
Colonel L E Coker RFA was appointed officer Commanding. The Brigade was called the 176th (Leicester) RFA Howitzer Brigade, and had its Head Quarters at the Leicester Football Club Ground, Aylestone Rd Leicester. About 90% of the men were recruited from the town of Leicester and its vicinity.

176th Brigade R.F.A.
Vol II

34

WAR DIARY
or
INTELLIGENCE SUMMARY

Army Form C. 2118

Place	Date	Hour	Summary of Events and Information	Remarks and references to Appendices
Leicester	28/5/15		Major Heygate joined the Brigade.	
"	1/6/15		Colonel L E Cotton joined, to take command of the Brigade.	
"	3/6/15		Officers Pro Temp. G W Heading Fawnik, E R Kent, C R Wickham joined the Brigade.	
"	4/6/15		2nd Lieut. J. Hudgens joined the Brigade, and took over Adjutant. Recruiting Commenced.	
"	7/6/15			
"	10/6/15		2nd Lieut. J. Arnold joined the Brigade.	
"	13/6/15		2nd Lieut. H W Bawtry joined the Brigade.	
"	17/6/15		2nd Lieut. H W Palfreyman and 0L Cartwright joined the Brigade.	mo
"	21/6/15		Recruiting (Officers) finished, the Brigade being complete to 25 Officers.	
"	24/6/15		Brigade inspected by His Grace, The Duke of Rutland, on the Leicester Rugby Football Ground. Present on parade (being the number chosen) 650 NCOs & men.	
"	29/6/15		2nd Lieut J Slatter joined the Brigade.	
"	29/6/15		Major Gustrad Williams and Brigadier General Edmunds CB inspected the Brigade.	

Army Form C. 2118

WAR DIARY
or
INTELLIGENCE SUMMARY
(Erase heading not required.)

Instructions regarding War Diaries and Intelligence Summaries are contained in F.S. Regs., Part II. and the Staff Manual respectively. Title Pages will be prepared in manuscript.

Place	Date	Hour	Summary of Events and Information	Remarks and references to Appendices
Leicester	July 5		Major J Datty joined the Brigade and took Command of B Battery.	
"	9		2/Lieut - R.Y.K. Walker joined the Brigade and took Command of A Battery.	
"	9		2/Lieut - Mr L Willis joined the Brigade.	
"	9		The first 100 horses arrived.	
"	13		1. 4.5 QF Howitzer arrived.	
"	23rd		2. 4.5 QF Howitzers arrived.	
"	24		2/Lieut - F H Webb joined the Brigade.	
"	26		2/Lieut - J H Godbr joined the Brigade.	
"	29th		1. 4.5 QF Howitzer arrived.	
"	Aug 1st		Col L E Coker granted 2 months sick leave.	
"	2nd		Brigade dismounted sports held on Leicester Rugby Football Ground. Mounted display held on Aulsy Park.	
"	3rd			
"	9		Col G.R.T. Runville CB joined and took Command of the Brigade.	

Army Form C. 2118

Instructions regarding War Diaries and Intelligence Summaries are contained in F.S. Regs., Part II. and the Staff Manual respectively. Title Pages will be prepared in manuscript.

WAR DIARY
or
INTELLIGENCE SUMMARY

(Erase heading not required.)

Place	Date	Hour	Summary of Events and Information	Remarks and references to Appendices
Leicester	Aug 16		2/Lieuts C Willett and A Wright joined the Brigade.	
"	19		Major M. Hartland Mahon joined the Brigade & took command of D Battery.	
"	20		Arrival of horses.	
"	23		40 N.C.O's and men under Lieut-Shakes proceeded to Tidworth Park with an advanced party.	
"	30		The Brigade left Leicester for Tidworth Park by Batteries at intervals of 2 hours, the first Battery leaving the L.C. Barracks station at 7.45 am.	
Tidworth Park	30		The Brigade marched in two strong recd and men.	
"	Sept 16		34th Divisional Artillery paraded for inspection by Gen. Sir A Paget.	
"	16		2/Lieut - S J Pickards joined the Brigade.	
"	18		2/Lieut - J R & Thom joined the Brigade.	

Army Form C. 2118

WAR DIARY
or
INTELLIGENCE SUMMARY
(Erase heading not required.)

Instructions regarding War Diaries and Intelligence Summaries are contained in F.S. Regs., Part II. and the Staff Manual respectively. Title Pages will be prepared in manuscript.

Place	Date	Hour	Summary of Events and Information	Remarks and references to Appendices
Hounslow Park	Sept 22nd		Lieut Winter promoted Temporary Captain.	
"	27th		2/Lieut Lloyd transferred to 5th Reserve Regt Cavalry.	
"	28th		2/Lieut Bluitt and two other ranks proceeded to Brighton Camp Certified as advance party.	
"	Oct 2nd		Brigade left Hounslow Park for Brighton Camp, strength 100 Ofrs 845 ORs. Marching in strength 11 Officers and 711 NCO & men.	
"	"		2/Lieut Westhead 30 NCO & men remained as Rearparty Hounslow Camp	
30/15 Camp H	4th		2/Lieut Harris Jones joined the Brigade.	
"	5th		The Rear party under 2/Lieut Webb arrived.	
"	9th		Lieut Mordan AVC arrived and was attached to the Brigade.	
"	22nd		Capt. Vernon Taylor RAMC arrived and was attached to the Brigade.	

Army Form C. 2118

WAR DIARY
or
INTELLIGENCE SUMMARY

(Erase heading not required.)

176 Bd R.F.A

Instructions regarding War Diaries and Intelligence Summaries are contained in F.S. Regs., Part II. and the Staff Manual respectively. Title Pages will be prepared in manuscript.

Place	Date	Hour	Summary of Events and Information	Remarks and references to Appendices
BOYTON	Nov 3rd	—	Divisional Field Day in WYLYE district-	
	Nov 4		A Battery took part on the first day, B Battery on the second day. B Battery field thank ammunition for the first time.	jegt jegt
	Nov 5		Divisional Route March. Route :- WARMINSTER – POINT 590 – BOWLS BARROW – HEYTESBURY. Iron Carriers received.	jegt
	Nov 12		Divisional Route March with billeting scheme at FONTHILL GIFFORD cancelled during the march, owing to bad weather.	jegt
	Nov 13		Two guns received	jegt
	Nov 18		Five guns received	jegt
	Nov 24		Inspection by G.O.C. R.A of batteries at Drill order Parade	jegt
			Remainder of guns received	jegt
	Nov 25		Divisional Exercise in MONKTON DEVERILL district.	jegt
	Nov 30		Divisional Exercise Route march with billeting scheme.	jegt
	Dec 6th		Gun Practice TILSHEAD	jegt
	Dec 10		Gun Practice TILSHEAD	jegt
	Dec 11		Gun Practice TILSHEAD	jegt
	Dec 12		Orders received re mobilization and preparation for service in EGYPT	jegt
	Dec 13		1st day of Mobilization	jegt
	Dec 14		2nd day of Mobilization	jegt
	Dec 15		3rd day of Mobilization	jegt
	Dec 16		4th day of Mobilization	jegt

176th Bde. R.F.A.
Vol. I

XXIV

Jan '16
Aug '16

WAR DIARY
or
INTELLIGENCE SUMMARY
(Erase heading not required.)

Army Form C. 2118

176th Bde. R.F.A.

Place	Date	Hour	Summary of Events and Information	Remarks and references to Appendices
BOYTON	Dec 20th		Capt BARTLEY joined the brigade and is posted to command C Battery	1904
	Dec 30th		Capt BISHOP joined the brigade and is posted to command B Battery	1904
1916	Jan 1st		Capt FERGUSON joined the brigade and is posted to command C Battery	1904
			Capt BARTLEY to transferred to command Ammunition Column	1904
	Jan 3rd		1st day of Mobilization for FRANCE	1904
			2nd Lieut MASON joined the brigade and is posted to D Battery	
	Jan 4th		2nd day of Mobilization	1904
			2nd Lieut YOUNG joined the brigade and is posted to A Battery	1904
	Jan 5th		3rd day of Mobilization	1904
	Jan 6th		4th day of Mobilization	1904
	Jan 7th		5th day of Mobilization	1904
	Jan 8th		Brigade entrained at CODFORD for SOUTHAMPTON where it entrained. Ship sailed 6.40 p.m. SOUTHAMPTON	1904
LE HAVRE	Jan 9th		Arrived LE HAVRE commenced disembarking 2 p.m. HQ Staff and A Battery entrained, remainder went to Rest Camp for the night	1904

WAR DIARY
INTELLIGENCE SUMMARY
(Erase heading not required.)

Army Form C. 2118

176/73de. R.F.A.

Place	Date	Hour	Summary of Events and Information	Remarks and references to Appendices
INGHEM	Jan 11th		The horses of B Battery Shampooed, Polyarsenic.	Appx
	Jan 12th		25 horses received	Appx
	Jan 13th		2 horses received	Appx
	Jan 17th		3 horses received	Appx
	Jan 19th		2nd Lieut. BELL joined the Brigade and was posted to D Battery	Appx
	Jan 20th		8 horses received	Appx
	Jan 21st			Appx
BLARINGHEM	Jan 23rd		The Brigade marched to BLARINGHEM	Appx
	Jan 24th		Lieut GREEN joined the Brigade and was posted to C Battery	Appx
			Lieut MACDONALD joined the Brigade and was posted to B Battery	Appx
	Jan 25th		Colonel G.R.T. Rundle CB. visited the 23rd Division in the forward area	Appx
	Jan 26th		4 Officers, 32 NCOs' and men, proceeded to horses from 73 BLARINGHEM for four days attachment to 23rd Division	Appx
	Jan 29th		1 Officer, 11 NCO's and men proceeded for attachment to 23rd Division	Appx
	Jan 30th		2 Battery Commanders, 4 Officers, H NCOs and men proceeded for attachment to 23rd Division. Previous parties returned.	Appx

G.R.T. Rundle
Colonel
O/C 176th Bde. R.F.A.

Army Form C. 2118

WAR DIARY
INTELLIGENCE SUMMARY
(Erase heading not required.)

176 Brigade R.F.A.

Place	Date	Hour	Summary of Events and Information	Remarks and references to Appendices
BLARINGHEM	3/5/16		Colonel Capt Rundle, two Battery Commanders, two officers & 42 O.R. proceeded for attachment 23rd D.W.	9CA
	4/5/16		B Batt. proceeded S./ BETHUNE for permanent attachment to 47th Dvn.	9CA
	7/5/16		3 officers & 9 O.R. proceeded for attachment 23rd Dvn.	9CA
	11/5/16	10 a.m.	A Battery was inspected by LORD KITCHENER at MORBECQUE	9CA
	13/5/16		A Batt. R.1 Section, B Batt. proceeded to Wagon line of 105th Bde R.F.A.	9CA
	14/5/16		C Batt. proceeded to wagon line of 105th Bde R.F.A.	9CA
	15/5/16		1 Section, A Batt & 2, 1 Section B Batt took over gun sections of A & B Batts. 105th Bde respectively	9CA
	16/5/16		C Batt took over from C & D Batts 105th Bde R.F.A. HQ Staff proceeded to 105 Bde.	9CA
	17/5/16		Remaining Sections A & D Batts. proceeded through lines 105 Bde.	9CA
	18/5/16		BAC proceeded to forward position. Remainder of Brigade took up from 105 Bde R.F.A.	9CA
ARMENTIÈRES	19/5/16	10 a.m.	Lt. Col. Get Rhodes C.B. took command of Brigade. Troops very misty. Quiet day. A Battery shelled registration on known points	9CA
	20/5/16		Enemy Artillery shewed more than usual activity in BOIS GRENIER and L'ARMÉE districts. C Batt. fired 10 rounds at NINNANA LA FLEUR D'ECOSSE as retaliation. A Batt. fired 8 rounds at L.E MARSHL to relieve shelling on LA BOUTILLERIE. 1 Batt. checked registration on known points and LA FLEUR D'ECOSSE during the afternoon. BOIS GRENIER heavily shelled between 11a.m. & 3p.m. The enemy Barrage on street lines in BOIS GRENIER. The following retaliation was carried out:—	9CA
	21/5/16	10.15am	Moulton fired 12 rounds at BRIDOUX FORT I.31,d.0.3.	
		10.45am	fired 10 rounds at Batty at 01.a.8.2	
		11 am	fired 10 rounds at Batty at 01.a.8.2	
		11.15am		
		3.53 pm	fired 42 rounds at Batty at 01.c.3.8.	
		4.6 pm		

WAR DIARY
or
INTELLIGENCE SUMMARY

Army Form C. 2118

176 Brigade R.F.A.

Place	Date	Hour	Summary of Events and Information	Remarks and references to Appendices
ARMENTIERES	21/7/16	12.30pm	C/Batty fired 8 rounds on ENNETIERES	
		1.0pm	LAVALLÉE	JCA
		3.25		JCA
		3.30pm	ENNETIERES	JCA
	22/7/16	1.30pm	B/Batty. Two salvoes on Barrage trench D.H	
		2.35pm	Two ,, ,, ,, ,, D.A	
		4pm	B/Battery registered on the STATION I.27.a.10.0.	
			Short and mist all day.	
	23/7/16		Quiet day, Observation difficult. B/Batty. fired on STATION I.27.a.94 and houses at I.27.a64	
	23/7/16		A/B/ 39 H.E. firing 12 direct hits.	
	24/7/16		Quite bad for observation. C/Batt. fired 8 rounds at BREWERY I.22.c.8½.4½	JCA
			B/Batt. engaged dugouts in German Trenches at I.26.d.3.7. with A.O.O.	
		1pm	B/Batt. engaged dugouts in German Trenches at I.26.d.3.7. Considerable damage was done	
		2.15pm	30 rounds H.E. Rest he direct hit was obtained. Very front day.	JCA
			50 rounds ,, ,, he fired part he direct hit was obtained. Very front day.	JCA
			Two more to observe.	
	25/7/16		A/Batt. registered on O.2.a.37 and O.9.c.5.6	
	26/7/16	11am	C/Batt. retaliated with 4 rounds on I.2.a.2.6. Our shelling my support trenches	
		4.30pm	LAVALLÉE & ENNETIERES ,, 16 rounds on Mill I.55.c.0.5. and 2 hits on 3.9.	JCA
			STA MILL I.55.c.0.5. and 2 hits on 3.9.	
		8.15pm	C/Batt. fired on LA HAUSSOIE	
			A/Batt. fired 20 rounds at cuporte I.26.d.3.7 without getting a direct hit, but burst in album. The wire and parapet were badly damaged	JCA

Army Form C. 2118

WAR DIARY
or
INTELLIGENCE SUMMARY
(Erase heading not required.)

176 Brigade RFA

Instructions regarding War Diaries and Intelligence Summaries are contained in F.S. Regs., Part II. and the Staff Manual respectively. Title Pages will be prepared in manuscript.

Place	Date	Hour	Summary of Events and Information	Remarks and references to Appendices
ARMENTIERES	27/1/16	4.15 pm	C Batt: checked registration on house I 29 d 2,4	A⁄C⁄9
			D Batt: fired 10 rounds on house I 3 2 c.	A⁄C⁄9
	28/1/16	4 pm	A Bat: fired 20 rounds at enemy observation station O 13 b 5.1. x O 13 d 39 as retaliation for shelling of BOIS GRENIER	
	29/1/16	11.30 am	A Batt: engaged guns at O 13 b 6 6½.6 and O 14 & 3 7.	
		12.0 noon	B eng'd OP N 23 a 7.4 gained direct hits	
		2.50 pm	Retaliation was carried out by D Batt'y for shelling trenches I 31.4	
		12.15 pm	C Batt: fired 75 rounds. 25 rounds were fired at house at I 29 & 2.8 and I 29 a Q.2. in the house which was obtained. 10 rounds were fired as retaliation for firing by L'ARMÉE	A⁄C⁄
		4.35 pm	One NCO of D Battery was killed. 10" H.B. 98 vines	

E. Rundle
Colonel
O/C 176 Bde RFA

176 RFA
vol 3

WAR DIARY or INTELLIGENCE SUMMARY

Army Form C. 2118

176 Brigade R.F.A.

Place	Date	Hour	Summary of Events and Information	Remarks and references to Appendices
ARMENTIERES	1/5/16		C Batt. Fired 16 rounds on DISTILLERIE and MILL. B Batt. fired 18 rounds on DISTILLERIE gained 6 direct hits. A Batt. Carried out retaliation and fired in active hostile batteries in conjunction with 4th Posn. R.F.A.	ppt
	2/5/16		A Batt. Shelled a battery for retaliation for shelling our support trenches. B Batt. Retaliated with 8 rounds on LE MAISNIL. C Batt. Fired 5 rounds in retaliation but d. am too hasty for observation. also 6 rounds were fired for retaliation.	ppt
	3/5/16		C Batt. Carried out a shoot in conjunction with left group. Fired 20 rounds at ESTAMINET DE LA BARRIERE, 5 rounds at FERM LA CORNE and 15 minutes at SHUTTER HOUSE.	ppt
	4/5/16		About 80 rounds & 2 fired in the neighbourhood of ARMENTIERES STATION. B Batt. fired 20 rounds at ES COBECQUES in retaliation. C Batt. fired 8 rounds during the afternoon.	ppt
	5/5/16		C Batt. Carried out retaliation some 39 rounds. B Batt. fired 16 rounds.	ppt
	6/5/16		C Batt. fired 19 rounds in retaliation for shelling our trenches. C Batt. Carried out a shoot into left group, fired 20 rounds at trenches. Were shifted in nr of CROIX ROUGE I.10.4.9 with 102 rounds 5-9" and 8". A Batt. fired 10 rounds into CROIX ROUGE O.26.d.9.7 and C Batt 12 into CAPPINGHEM on retaliation. also B Batt 10 rounds into ESCOBECQUES.	ppt
	7/5/16			ppt
	8/5/16		B Batt. carried out shoot A fires 12 rds. at Trap I.26 & 7.1.	ppt

Army Form C. 2118

WAR DIARY
or
INTELLIGENCE SUMMARY
(Erase heading not required.)

176th Brigade R.F.A.

Place	Date	Hour	Summary of Events and Information	Remarks and references to Appendices
ARMENTIERES	9/3/16		A Batt. fired 23 in retaliation in conjunction with C Bat. R.G.A.	grd
	10/3/16		Batt. retaliated on enemy support trenches with 20 rounds.	grd
			No rounds fired. Enemy fired between 30 and 40 77mm at BOIS GRENIER line. Capt. S.C. BARTLEY took over temporary command of B Batt.	grd
	11/3/16		No rounds fired.	grd
	12/3/16		Enemy fired 56mm to 4.2" into BOIS GRENIER during the morning and another 26 during the afternoon. We retaliated on RADINGHEM. Capt. S.C. BARTLEY killed by shell in BOIS GRENIER.	grd
	13/3/16	2 pm	B Batt. carried out scheme firing 41 HE, at the head of a communication trench. A large punch to the enemy parapet was made and the communication trench behind into which we fired for some distance broken. A & C Batts. curtailed to 3 Sh per Gun the day's ammunition to be fired with aeroplane but it was too misty for observation. A&C Batts. to fire into SHAFTESBURY AVENUE and CHAPELLE D'ARMENTIERES who shelled Rue du marais with 77 mm and 4.2.	grd
	14/3/16		Enemy heavy trench mortar fired R.R.3 into COUZON. We retaliated but 10 rounds into Enemy parapet unsuccessful retaliation with an aeroplane.	grd
	15/3/16		A Batt. after carried out successful retaliation #152 Batt. aimed too much 5.9 into Point between gables. (6.2. 31 Bn. on our left. The trench mortar heavy shelled a trifler of 18pdrs undergone, a direct hit was obtained on one of our guns. The gun was only damaged in the front, the retaliated with 5 rounds at ERQUINGHEM.	grd
	16/3/16	9.10 am		grd

WAR DIARY
or
INTELLIGENCE SUMMARY
(Erase heading not required.)

Army Form C. 2118

176"Bde R.F.A

Place	Date	Hour	Summary of Events and Information	Remarks and references to Appendices
ARMENTIERES	17/3/16		Very misty day. Very quiet day.	root
	18/3/16		Dull day. Very little firing. A Batt fired 4 rounds. Lt. of Whittington in to aeroplane	root
	19/3/16		CAPT. R.W. ARDAGH joined the Brigade and was posted to command D Batt.	root
			Martin fired 40 rounds during the day.	
			C Batty fired 20 rounds at the RE Dump trenches at WEZ MACQUART by aeroplane	root
			12 rounds of these were blind.	root
	20/3/16		Very misty. Artillery very quiet during the day.	root
	21/3/16		Very quiet. Colonel DAVEY and Lieut. McALEERY J.C. attached for 14 days instruction	root
	22/3/16		No firing. Mist all day	root
	23/3/16		B Bat fired 12 rounds. C Bat 5 rounds. The gun of B Batt away for repairs returned.	root
	24/3/16		No firing. Too misty to observe anything.	root
	25/3/16		Snow. Dull all day. No firing.	root
	26/3/16		8 men of A Bratt moved into the night on relief of B Bratt. where 57 Wpate. was	
			8 men of A Batt to B Batt. other sections of A Batt relieved remaining section of B Batt	1002
	27/3/16		A Bat fired 13 rounds in retaliation for shelling from 15 pdr battery and a part of	1003
			Couverture. kept by troop.	
	28/3/16		20 rounds fired by troop.	
	29/3/16		Very windy. No firing.	root
	30/3/16		B Bat. fired 20 rounds. A.C Batt 5 rounds. About 22 rounds a.C Batt 5 rounds.	root
	31/3/16		35 rounds fired.	root

H.P.Burne
Colonel
O/C 176"Bde C.R.A.

Army Form C. 2118

WAR DIARY
or
INTELLIGENCE SUMMARY
(Erase heading not required.)

176. Bde. R.F.A. Vol 4

XXXIV

Place	Date	Hour	Summary of Events and Information	Remarks and references to Appendices
ARMENTIERES	April 1st to April 8th		Normal registration and retaliation carried out. Total number of rounds fired during week 430. On April 4th two officers and 30 men of the battery were detached for instruction. Another officer arrived to arrange an attachment on the 7th. On April 5th 30 officers and 9 men were attached to HQ staff for instruction. 2nd Lieut. G. C. WINGROVE arrived and joined A Battery.	Sgd/
	April 9th to April 15th		Normal registration carried out. 1st April. This week, April 11th orders were received to help first part of the Australians. 500 rounds have been allowed for the instruction of the Australians.	Sgd/
	April 16th		Capt. W. F. ROBERTSON joined the brigade and was posted to command the B/176.	Sgd/
	April 16th to April 22nd		Normal registration and retaliation carried out in a very small degree. Instruction of Australians continued. Each battery was relieved by 2 Australian one section of each battery.	Sgd/
	April 22nd to April 23rd		Headquarters section relieved. Brigade marched to arms, Trayssy area, arrived HAVERSKERQUE and billeted there.	Sgd/

Army Form C. 2118

WAR DIARY
or
INTELLIGENCE SUMMARY
(Erase heading not required.)

Instructions regarding War Diaries and Intelligence Summaries are contained in F.S. Regs., Part II. and the Staff Manual respectively. Title Pages will be prepared in manuscript.

Place	Date	Hour	Summary of Events and Information	Remarks and references to Appendices
QUELMES	24/3/16		Bde. marched from MAVERSKERQUE, starting 8 a.m. arrived QUELMES 6 p.m.	Appx
	25/3/16		Training Carried out.	Appx
	26/3/16		" " "	Appx
	29/3/16		2/Lt. H.S. BELL joined the Brigade and posted to B/176	

[signature]
for Colonel,
Commanding 176th Brigade, R.F.A.

WAR DIARY or INTELLIGENCE SUMMARY

Army Form C. 2118

XXIV — 176th F.A. Bde.

Place	Date	Hour	Summary of Events and Information	Remarks and references to Appendices
QUELMES	1/5/16 to 4/5/16		Brigade training	Appx
	5/5/16		Brigade entrained at WIZERNES and ST OMER	Appx
	6/5/16		Brigade detrained at LONGUEAU and marched to BEAUCOURT	Appx
	6/6/16		Brigade marched to ALBERT and bivouacked the night at the wagon lines	Appx
	7/5/16		Reorganisation of Brigade Artillery. Brigade Ammunition Column split up	Appx
	8/5/16		Reorganisation of Brigade Artillery. Brigade split up. Batteries transferred	Appx
ALBERT	14/5/16		and renumbered as follows:-	Appx
			(a) A/176 transferred to 160th Bde. B/152	
			C/176 152nd Bde. D/160	
			D/176 175th Bde. C/175	
	21/5/16		(b) A/176 new designation A/176	
			C/176 — B/176	
			D/176 — C/175	
			Of the new batteries C Battery was in action, the other two digging gun pits	

WAR DIARY
or
INTELLIGENCE SUMMARY

Army Form C. 2118

176th Brigade R.F.A.

Place	Date	Hour	Summary of Events and Information	Remarks and references to Appendices
ALBERT	2/5/16		The new Batteries consisted of the following Officers:- A Battery B Battery C Battery Capt. H.H. BAXTER Major A.K. MAIN Capt. G.T. SPANN Lieut. G. HOWITT 2/Lieut. S.W. PUMPHREY Lieut. R. THORP 2/Lieut. J.R. BUDD — T.R. SEWELL 2/Lieut. T. PAYNE — D. WALLIS — G.W. BOWMAN 2/Lieut. A.B. MACDONALD — G. FERNIE — 18H NELSON — M.H. THOMAS	
	2/5/16 to 31/5/16		None. Registration and retaliation carried out by C Battery. Remainder of batteries digging gun pits.	
	30/5/16		One gun of 4/176 out of action. Replaced in the night with a gun of 15/176.	

J. Richmond Lt. for Colonel,
Commanding 176th Brigade, R.F.A.

WAR DIARY or **INTELLIGENCE SUMMARY**
(Erase heading not required.)

Army Form C. 2118

June
176 RFA
XXXIV
Vol 6

Place	Date	Hour	Summary of Events and Information	Remarks and references to Appendices
ALBERT	1/6/16		C Battery in action in AUTHUILE WOOD, the other two Batteries preparing gun positions in TARA VALLEY	
	5/6/16			
	2/6/16		C Battery called upon to capture in stopping enemy raid on our trenches	
	3/6/16		C Battery upon called for him help and	
	4/6/16		C Battery covered by firing a barrage to cover a successful raid on enemy trenches	
	5/6/16		No less than each of A&B Batteries relieved section of 175 F.A. one Battery	
	7/6/16		Each of the sections completed. Three of the Batteries fired part of June	
	9/6/16		The hopp. this dint	
			1 RFA Billet in C Battery. This was the Battery's first crossing	
	10/6/16		A & B Batteries took their turn at taking to their new positions	
	15/6/16		Registration for wire cutting was carried out by our Batteries from these	
	16/6/16		dates onwards	
	24/6/16		Bombardment started. Wire cutting was carried out by Batteries	
			Special fire carried out at night on enemy communication trenches	
			Shoots which were fired A 311 B 688 C 553 I.R.P to Batteries blue & mauve	
	25/6/16		Bombardments and wire cutting carried out according to scheme also the carrying	
			Shoots which were fired A 600 B 1134 C 1327	
	26/6/16		4 am & 6.24am Special bombardment of enemy trenches	
			Bombardments wire cutting and night fire carried out according to scheme	
			By I.R.P B Btys fire billets to fire at one	
			Shoots made fired during the day A 794 B 1193 C 1612	

Army Form C. 2118

WAR DIARY
or
INTELLIGENCE SUMMARY
(Erase heading not required.)

Instructions regarding War Diaries and Intelligence Summaries are contained in F.S. Regs., Part II. and the Staff Manual respectively. Title Pages will be prepared in manuscript.

Place	Date	Hour	Summary of Events and Information	Remarks and references to Appendices
ALBERT	27/6/16		Bombardment, wire cutting and night firing continued Scheme A 1280 B 1134 C 1608. The following minds were fired.	
	28/6/16		Bombardment, wire cutting and night firing continued Scheme A 1108 B 1096 C 1811. The following minds were fired. Lieut F.S. MISBURGH junior to Captn. M.H. BAXTER and 2nd/Lt R. wounded. Take command of A Battery and promoted Captain. Bombardment, wire cutting and night firing carried out according to scheme.	
	29/6/16		No flights made were fired A 444 B 810 C 511. Heavy bombardment 4 pm to 5.6 pm. Special bombardment should have relieved in this day, but was postponed owing to bad weather.	
	30/6/16		Last day of Bombardment. Special bombardment 12.40 pm to 3.30 pm. Bombardment, wire cutting and night firing carried out according to scheme. The following minds were fired A 1096 B 793 C 409. During the bombardment at no time four guns were out of action at the same time in one Bty. Prior to 11th inst with the Bde. Spring on the night of June 30th all guns of the Bde. were in action. Considerable trouble was experienced with the Buffer Springs.	

J.R.P. Crundley
Lt. Col
O/c 6" Bde R.G.A

1875 Wt. W593/826 1,000,000 4/15 J.B.C. & A. A.D.S.S./Forms/C. 2118.

Army Form N. 1531A.
(To be made out in duplicate.)

FOR USE IN THE FIELD.

ACCOUNT of sums received and expended by the Sub-Accountant during the month of _April_ 1916, in account with the

Paymaster _____

Paymaster's Ledger Folio _____

Dr.

Date	No. of Voucher	From whom received	Particulars	Francs Amount £ s. d.
April 2nd	Book 1	Field Cashier 11 Corps	Coquingham	700
	RFA/1029			
" 9		do	Croisselles Bac	500
" 16		do	do	400
" 20		do	Armentières	400
			Carried forward Total Receipts	2000
			Balance due to Paymaster on last Account	
			Balance due by Paymaster on this Account	
			TOTAL DR.	

Cr.

Date	No. of Voucher	To whom paid	Particulars	Francs Amount £ s. d.
April 3rd	30			260
" 3rd	31			125
" "	32			20
" "	33			40
" 6	34			10
" 9	35			255
" "	36			175
" 10	37			20
" 11	38			100
" "	39			130
" "	40			225
" "	41			60
" "	42			10
" "	43			50
" "	44			160
" 21	45			95
			Carried forward Total Expenditure	1745
			Balance due by Paymaster on last Account	
			Balance due to Paymaster on this Account	
			TOTAL CR.	

I certify that the above Account is correct.

_____ Sub-Accountant.

Station and Date _____

1. This Account is to be made out by the Sub-Accountant (the vouchers supporting the several credits and charges being annexed and numbered as "Sub-Vouchers") and should be forwarded as soon after end of month as possible, to the A. G. at the Base, who will transmit it to the Paymaster concerned at the earliest opportunity.
2. When this Form is used by the General Staff in connection with intelligence duties, the Sub-Accountant shall attach a Certificate in those cases where it is not possible or expedient to obtain Vouchers.
3. Vouchers or Certificates should be numbered 1, 2, 3, &c.

Army Form N. 1531A.
(To be made out in duplicate.)

Forms N.1531A./2

Wt. W1856—9. 7,500 Bks. 8/14. D.L.R.& Co. Ltd.

FOR USE IN THE FIELD.

ACCOUNT of sums received and expended by the Sub-Accountant during the month of April 1916, in account with the

Paymaster _____ Paymaster's Ledger Folio _____

Dr.

Date	No. of Voucher	From whom received	Particulars	Amount (francs)
			Brought forward	2000
			Total Receipts	2000 francs
			Balance due to Paymaster on last Account	
			Balance due by Paymaster on this Account	
			TOTAL DR.	2000 francs

Cr.

Date	No. of Voucher	To whom paid	Particulars	Amount (francs)
April 21st	46		Brought forward	1745
" 21	47			10
" 28	48	As per list attached		30
				20 3.25
				2
			Total Expenditure	1828.25
			Balance due by Paymaster on last Account	143.50
			Balance due to Paymaster on this Account	28.25
			TOTAL CR.	2000 francs

Station and Date B.E.F. April 30

I certify that the above Account is correct.

R. C. Rom 2/Lt. R.F.A.
Sub-Accountant.

Adjutant 176th Brigade, R.F.A.

the vouchers supporting the several credits and charges being annexed and numbered as "Sub-Vouchers"

1. This Account is to be made out by the Sub-Accountant (the vouchers supporting the several credits and charges being annexed and numbered as "Sub-Vouchers") and should be forwarded as soon after end of month as possible, to the A. G. at the Base, who will transmit it to the Paymaster concerned at the earliest opportunity.
2. When this Form is used by the General Staff in connection with intelligence duties, the Sub-Accountant shall attach a Certificate in those cases where it is not possible or expedient to obtain Vouchers.
3. Vouchers or Certificates should be numbered 1, 2, 3, &c.

Imprest Account no Wool 1/R.F.A./1029.

Army Form W. 3313.
(In Pads of 20.)

Identification No. 2

2nd Army — 34 — Division. — 176th — Brigade.

Week ending 30/4/1916

RETURN OF SUPPLIES purchased during week ending for H.Q. 176 Bde (Unit).

Date of Purchase	Rank and Name of Purchaser	Article	Quantity	Rate	Amount Paid Total F.	C.	Name of Vendor	Address of Vendor	Strength of Formation for which separate purchases have been made	Remarks
10/4/16	2nd Lieut J.R.G. Foon	Potatoes	20 Kilos	30 c	6	0	Repin	Aventin	50	
15/4/16	do	Potatoes	10 Kilos	30 c	3	0	Repin	Aventin	50	
20/4/16	do	Potatoes	5 Kilos	30 c	1	50	Repin	Montry	50	
25/4/16	do	Potatoes	75 Kilos	1.70	12	75	Ducamp	Ducamp	50	
					23	25				

Note.—Every article to be shown separately with its price. Only A.S.C. Supply Services to be shown on this form. Certified that no Requisition Receipt Note has been given for same.

Signature [signed]
2/Lt. R.F.A. (Bank).
Adjutant 176th Brigade, R.F.A. Corps.

Date 1/5/16

To D.D.S. & T. _____ Army.
A.D.S. & T. _____ Cavalry Corps.

I Certify that the within-mentioned purchases are necessary, and prices reasonable with the exception of _____

Date _____ 191__   Signature _____ A. S. C. Supply Officer.

Additional observations of the D.D.S. & T. Army or A.D.S. & T. Cavalry Corps, &c., to be made here.

_____

Signature _____

To Paymaster-in-Chief.

The within purchases are approved by me, except _____ which should in my opinion be disallowed. The following purchases should be allowed, only to the extent of _____

Signature _____ Director of Supplies.

20.5 pmditi a 30

6 Sd.

nage

regina

② 16/2/16

1 horloge provision de ... 3.00

Reçu Bégua

⑧ 25/4/14

prdt

1.5⁰

regina

From:- H.Q. 176th BRIGADE, R.F.A.

To:- A.G's Office 3rd Echelon

Secret

Herewith War Diary for 176th Brigade R.F.A. for the period 1/5/16 to 31/5/16.

2/6/16

[signature] Lt. for
Colonel,
Commanding 176th Brigade, R.F.A.

④ 25 avril 1916

Reçu pour 7f Kilos pommes de terre
à 12.75

J Ducamp

34th Div.
III.Corps.

WAR DIARY

Headquarters,

176th BRIGADE, R.F.A.

J U L Y

1 9 1 6

Army Form C. 2118.

Undated 7
176 Bde RFA (1)
Vol 7

34th DIVISION

WAR DIARY
OR
INTELLIGENCE SUMMARY.
(Erase heading not required.)

Instructions regarding War Diaries and Intelligence Summaries are contained in F.S. Regs., Part II. and the Staff Manual respectively. Title pages will be prepared in manuscript.

Place	Date	Hour	Summary of Events and Information	Remarks and references to Appendices
ALBERT	1/7/16	6.25am to 9.43am	Intensive bombardment of enemy's trenches, our Infantry attacking at 7.30 am. During the day barrages were maintained by our batteries. During the afternoon parties of the enemy were fired on by B Battery whilst returning to AELIGOLAND. Barrages were kept up during the night. One O.R. B Battery wounded by premature. Rounds fired A/176 1260 B/176 1475 C/176 1318	
	2/7/16		Barrages maintained throughout day and night. During the period of taking LA BOISSELLE, the enemy were fired at with good effect by batteries. When the 19th Division were advancing across the open the enemy were seen to man a trench S. of LA BOISSELLE. C Battery immediately opened fire on them and enfiladed the trench. The trench was cleared by their advance at about half an hour after this trench was occupied by 19th Division in front of cavalry. Rounds fired A/176 1286 B/176 1307 C/176 2045	

Army Form C. 2118.

176 Bde F4 (2)

34th DIVISION

WAR DIARY
or
INTELLIGENCE SUMMARY.
(Erase heading not required.)

Instructions regarding War Diaries and Intelligence Summaries are contained in F. S. Regs., Part II. and the Staff Manual respectively. Title pages will be prepared in manuscript.

Place	Date	Hour	Summary of Events and Information	Remarks and references to Appendices
ALBERT	3/7/16		Barrages maintained day and night. Whilst 19th Division were bombing trenches in LA BOISSELLE, the enemy were seen to man a communication trench 200 yards N. of LA BOISSELLE. Sniping at our bombers. The enemy were engaged by C Battery and the trench was cleared. This trench was occupied by 19th Division but few casualties. A party of enemy retreated was fired upon during the afternoon by B Battery. Rounds expended M/176 1120. B/176 812. C/176 1264.	
	4/7/16		Barrages maintained day and night. At about noon the enemy were observed manning a trench N.W. of LA BOISSELLE. Sniping at our bombers. They were engaged by C Battery with excellent effect. The trench being cleared. An infantry attack this time was made on the trenches from the front. C Battery continued sniping the enemy whenever he showed himselves. Rounds expended. M/176 1118. B/176 1311. C/176 644.	
	5/7/16		Barrages maintained day and night. C Battery continued sniping the enemy. Rounds expended M/176 859. B/176 1831. C/176 392.	

Army Form C. 2118.

176 Bde F.A (13)

WAR DIARY
or
INTELLIGENCE SUMMARY.
(Erase heading not required.)

Place	Date	Hour	Summary of Events and Information	Remarks and references to Appendices
ALBERT	6/7/16		Barrages maintained day and night. Battn. relieved by 19th Division and retired through into to join the whole Group. Rounds expended A/176 587 B/176 1098	
	7/7/16	10am	Bombardment in second phase of attack. After attack barrages were maintained day and night. Rounds expended A/176 1414 B/176 1501	
	8/7/16		Barrages maintained. Lieut. Colonel E.B. COTTER Joined the Brigade. Rounds expended A/176 353 B/176 1194	
	9/7/16 10/7/16		Barrages maintained. Rounds expended A/176 607 A/176 1412 B/176 544 B/176 942 Colonel G.R.T. RUNDLE C.B. R.A. departed for ENGLAND. Lieut. Colnel E.B. COTTER took Command of the Brigade. Major A.K. MAIN transferred to Hd. Qrs. 34th Division. Lieut. J. O'CALLAGHAN posted to Command B/176.	

Army Form C. 2118.

176 Bde F17 (4)

WAR DIARY
or
INTELLIGENCE SUMMARY.
(Erase heading not required.)

Place	Date	Hour	Summary of Events and Information	Remarks and references to Appendices
ALBERT	11/7/16		Barrage maintained on enemy's position 1000ˣ S.E. of LA BOISSELLE. Rounds expended A/176 728 B/176 569	
	12/7/16		A & B Batteries fire at extreme ranges, being Reft. in their old position for defensive purposes. Rounds expended A/176 248 B/176 80 B Battery commenced work on forward position.	
	13/7/16 14/7/16		No firing except of Rounds expended A/176 89 B/176 nil A & B Batteries maintained special barrages to cover attack on Hght and Left of POZIERES. Rounds expended A/176 435 B/176 243.	
	15/7/16 16/7/16		C Battery moved one gun forward into new position in SAUSAGE VALLEY. A Battery quiet day. Shelled on POZIERES all night. Ammunition expended 21SA & 76AX B Battery one other rank wounded by premature while working on forward position. C Battery in action in forward position.	
	17/7/16		A Battery bombards POZIERES rounds expended AX23, A155, B Battery fire a barrage A101, AX 22. C continue work in forward position.	

Army Form C. 2118.

176/Bde/FA(5)

WAR DIARY
or
INTELLIGENCE SUMMARY
(Erase heading not required.)

Instructions regarding War Diaries and Intelligence Summaries are contained in F. S. Regs., Part II. and the Staff Manual respectively. Title pages will be prepared in manuscript.

Place	Date	Hour	Summary of Events and Information	Remarks and references to Appendices
ALBERT	18/7/16		A & B. batteries move into forward position & register their Zone. B. Battery have 2 horses killed & one wounded by premature. Both batteries work all night on their new positions.	
	19/7/16		Work done on new O.P.s. Ammunition expended. A/Batty. AX 14, A 340, B.batty. 36A71AX	
	20/7/16		Registering continued, 9 work on comforts. Ammunition expended by A batty AX 44, A 419. B.batty A 95, AX 18. Germans shoot over a great number of gas shells in early hours & kernes. German fire heavy on Australian infantry just in front of battery. A battery forced to take cover. A battery fires rapid bursts of fire when 900 horses were seen. Ammunition expended A 66, AX 62.	
	21/7/16		Heavy German fire in preparation for attack on POZIÈRES. G.12" C.Battery takes part in preparation for attack on POZIÈRES. German Barrage, C Batty La. 1 injured, 2 Howitzers wounded. Australians succeed by premature. Ammunition expended AX 72, A 76.	
	22/7/16		A Battery has one man wounded by premature. Ammunition expended AX 47, A 161	
	23/7/16		Brigade fire all night on POZIÈRES. Ammunition expended AX 93, A 446. Quiet day. Brigade fire all night on POZIÈRES. Ammunition expended AX 93, A 446.	
	24/7/16.		Attack on POZIÈRES by Australians which was successful.	

Army Form C. 2118.

176 BdeF.A (6)

WAR DIARY
or
INTELLIGENCE SUMMARY.
(Erase heading not required.)

Date	Hour	Summary of Events and Information	Remarks and references to Appendices
23/7/16		Very heavy bombardment of POZIERES by Germans who made several counter attacks all unsuccessful. The largest buffer of fire A.x.24, A.1090. Lt G. Howitt Leaves A battery. 2.L attached to Brigade Headquarters	
24/7/16		2Lt TUDHOPE in charge of A battery. The Brigade fires a barrage behind POZIERES A.x.193, A.572	
27/7/16		Barrage fires again. Ammunition expended A.x.191, A.720.	
28/7/16		A quiet day	
29/7/16		2Lt TUDHOPE and 2 other ranks of A battery wounded at CONTALMAISON, brigade fires a barrage at night, enemy fires A.x.169, A 634	
30/7/16	12pm	B battery fires A 151. A.x.46, a barrage N.E. of POZIERES in the early morning. at 12 noon A & B battery are back. B barrage fire for new overhead fire before being a battery fires 720A & 79 A.x, batteries more or not at 2 hours where no more have to move. There is at the same time. Enemy bombardment A battery area 20 guns of 150 kgs for an hour & all work very satisfactory. L. Battery have all been evacuated & are left in the line to be attached to the 160 Brigade.	

Army Form C. 2118.

176 Bde (FA(7))

WAR DIARY
or
INTELLIGENCE SUMMARY.
(Erase heading not required.)

Place	Date	Hour	Summary of Events and Information	Remarks and references to Appendices
	31/7/16		C Battery have a direct hit on the gun pit which blew several the gun & damaged the wheels, slide & a new gun is needed for. 2 Gunners are wounded. During the bombardment and the attack up till the last day of the month the Brigade fired A 42,584, and A X 12,471 rounds.	

J. Fisher Lt Col RFA
Comdg. 176th Bde RFA.

34th Divisional Artillery.

176th BRIGADE

ROYAL FIELD ARTILLERY

AUGUST 1 9 1 6:::

Army Form C. 2118.

WAR DIARY
INTELLIGENCE SUMMARY.
(Erase heading not required.)

176 F.A. Bde.

Place	Date	Hour	Summary of Events and Information	Remarks and references to Appendices
ALBERT.	1/8/16		AUGUST 1916. A battery moved back to the wagon lines & remained there till August 5 for a short rest for men & horses & also for a compleat overhaul of their guns & stores. B. battery also drew the same & remained at the wagon lines till Aug 6th 1916.	
	2/8/16		C. Battery remained in action goar (EAST OF BOISSELLE) & fired all day & night on barrages, varying rate of fire according to instructions received from Liason Officer & F.O.O.s concerning the movements of the enemy. C battery fired 987 Rounds.	
	3/8/16		The same work was carried on by C/176 & they fired	1464
			" " " " " " " " " "	603
	4/8/16	9.15.PM.	The Australians attacked the Fireworks. O.B.1 & O.B.2 in the evening of 4th wondered? N.E. of POZIÈRES & fired during the night	
	5/8/16		This was a quiet day as the guns had been that season wake?, heavy shelling at night. Hickory cops? opened fire at 6 rounds per gun per minute for one hour. C. Battery fired 522 Rounds.	1143 Rounds.
			C Battery fired 522 Rounds. A sprang? going through	
	6/8/16		H.2.? 9 gas shells causing slight medicalorage? Ammo fire by battery	654

WAR DIARY
INTELLIGENCE SUMMARY.
(Erase heading not required.)

Army Form C. 2118.

176 F.A. Bde.

Place	Date	Hour	Summary of Events and Information	Remarks and references to Appendices
Albert			During the rest of the day our Bde. A & B. Batteries have several practice rounds action, laying & direct gun drill. Section were taken by officers every day. The Brigade had competitions, A Battery won the one hour gun, smartest gun, and officers charge. The Brigade Head quarters were at rear from of Foris, & the Batteries. The G.O.C.R.A. & the Brigade Brig. inspected	
	Aug 5th			
	Aug 7.	6 A.M.	6/1/76 came into action for the army on our, Cherring the relief at German counter attacks N.E. of POZIÈRES & one section was kept in action to keep rifled shells attacks, the attack failed at section fire. 15"03 rounds	
			B/176 relieved B/160 during the morning & registered their lines of fire during the day on barrage road. 320 rounds	
			B/176 continued registering our targets & put on barrage and Cheffs on roads below the German front line also kept them from bringing up reinforcements & supplies to their front line. Enemies during the day 96 H rounds	
	8/8/16		A quiet day. My B/176 in action & Bty in a Q Lines at B 3 minutes	
	10/8/16		Left action of A/176 relieved left section of 113th Battery, 1st Div in a position west of MARLBORO WOOD & came under orders of 23rd Div.	

Army Form C. 2118.

176 F.A. Bde

WAR DIARY
or
INTELLIGENCE SUMMARY.
(Erase heading not required.)

Place	Date	Hour	Summary of Events and Information	Remarks and references to Appendices
ALBERT.	10/8/16		B/176 fired on the usual Barrages up till 8 P.M. when they were relieved by A/175- & proceeded to Wagon lines. The relief tk a long time as the position was being shelled & Cl. Gases. Horse & escort the fired before leaving. 759 rounds. B/176 proceed to Clear Wagon line. C/176 relieved in section of 115" Battery, 1st Div. F. of MARLBOROWOOD & fired by star lights. 364 rounds.	
	11/9/16		Remained section of A/176 relieves new Heavy section of 113" battery & fire on Carnoy. 926 rounds. B/176 our section relieve, the relieve of 114th Battery. 113" at MARLBOROWOOD's/ho. 593 rounds. C/176 The guns taken over from this Division were for eighteen & three due keppa covers then.	
	12/8/16		We attached cl. German scented bomb very successfully & the rest be buy with fired during the day in a Barrage behind Lt. German front line. at Bn. August fires. 3495 rounds. — A/176 = 1041, B= 575, C= 1450.	

Army Form C. 2118.

WAR DIARY
INTELLIGENCE SUMMARY.
(Erase heading not required.)

176 F.A. Bde.

Place	Date	Hour	Summary of Events and Information	Remarks and references to Appendices
	12/7/16		The 176 at Bignor H2 arrived up at the Head Quarters, just in front of Contalmaison.	
			A Cl. 1st Div NE of MAMETZ.	
	12/7/16		Gunner BUTCHER A/176 was wounded by a premature.	
	13/7/16		A/176 was shelled very heavy by 6" & 8" shells & closely enough they were	
			No battery came to take up the position they had vacated.	
			B/176 was relieved by C/234 & they relieved C/102 north of CONTALMAISON. The 375 was	
			have the following casualties	
	13/7/16		No 25702 Sgt ATKINSON. G. Wounded.	
			No 27632 . HOLDSWORTH.W ..	
	14/3/16		No 25516 Br DYSON W	
			Bde H20 moved to Fricourt and had a relay station in SHELTER WOOD on the	
	14/7/16		German dug out. German shell very heavily in front of our positions in	
			CATERPILLAR VALLEY. Renewing section of A/176 relieves A/103.	
			received fire from 64A & 16 AX.	

WAR DIARY
INTELLIGENCE SUMMARY.
(Erase heading not required.)

176 F.A. Bde.

Place	Date	Hour	Summary of Events and Information	Remarks and references to Appendices
	15/9/16		All batteries which have been registered on new trench GLOSTER ALLEY 7pm on barrage for rest of day & night. Rounds fired 2317	
	16/9/16		All batteries were in very carefully registered the SWITCH TRENCH & a very good work was done by all. During telephonic wire communications every heavy shelling. At 2 PM we only managed to connect on to Tapes. At 4 PM a barrage found on a barrage on the ELBOW & SWITCH TRENCH. B/176 casualties L7485 Gr. T. CONN Killed L1250 " J. HUDSON Wounded. One horse wounded & ammunition wagon smashed near battery position. Ammunition expended 2260.	
	17/9/16 7AM		Attack on SWITCH TRENCH by 15th Div. infantry after a hurricane bombardment in which our batteries assisted. The batteries left up a very rapid rate of fire & consequently suffered in air buffers. Rounds fired 3990	
	17/9/16 A/176		Casualty Gr. WESTMAN accidentally hit in his armoury at buffer. A spring flew back & became jambed & sliced, it was taking up ?? buffer. He after under loss of & cut him near the eye.	

Army Form C. 2118.

6

WAR DIARY
INTELLIGENCE SUMMARY.
(Erase heading not required.)

176 F.A. Bde.

Place	Date	Hour	Summary of Events and Information	Remarks and references to Appendices
CONTALMAISON	18/9/16		Barrages as ordered. 1 section of each battery was relieved by one section of the 50th Div Art. Rounds fired 245·F	
	19/9/16		The relieved section of each battery marched to Wagon Line at ALBERT. Barrage as ordered by evening. Section regularly fired sections at night. The left section was relieved by the R section of 50th Div & marry at Clay on the R section march back to BIENCT at FRICHENCOURT. The left section stay night at Wagon Line. The Brigade H.Q. been on 150th Div at 6 P.M. & march back to Wagon Line. Rounds fired 193F	
	20/9/16 21/9/16		Left Sections & Bdc H.Q. moved to Frichencourt. Br BENTLEY admitted to Hospital C/176 Brigade mess at FRICHENCOURT. March off at night independently to LONGEAU & return for FRICHENCOURT. The Bde H.Q. ahead at SAILLEUX	
	23/9/16 24/9/16		Batteries debus at BAILLEUL. One section of each battery moves out each day between ARMENTIÈRES and BOIS GRENIER & relief the 18th Div.	

WAR DIARY
INTELLIGENCE SUMMARY

Army Form C. 2118.

176 F.A. Bde.

Place	Date	Hour	Summary of Events and Information	Remarks and references to Appendices
ARMENTIERES	25/8/16		At ordinary stations general action registration checked & ammunition	
	26/8/16		C/176 had a horse also gun detonator result of shrapnel	
	27/8/16			
	28/8/16	12 Noon	RE-ORGANISATION of Brigade completed for day. 176th Bde. ceases to exist A/176 becomes A/152, which was old original man & is joined by R[T] & 9 C/176 making it a 6 gun batt[er]y. B/176 R[T] & transferred to A/160. & left & to B/160. C/176 R[T] Section to A/152. & Lieut. & to C/160. The 176 Bde H.Q. was after up taken at 152 & 160 batt[erie]s. The 178th Bde was originally the org HOWITZER Brigade in our division & on re-organization. being the fewer brigade of the div. it too had after up. As at 12 noon Aug 28/16 the 176th became second Harger Brigade & has taken up 9 officers & men now force Howr. battery & on made 6 gun batteries as follows.	

WAR DIARY
INTELLIGENCE SUMMARY.
(Erase heading not required.)

Army Form C.2118. 176 F.A. Bde.

Place	Date	Hour	Summary of Events and Information	Remarks and references to Appendices
176th Bde H.Q.			24/5/16 The present ed. Officers of the Brigade and posts are as follows. Lieut Colonel S.B.Bodle in charge of HQ. Brigade & ammunition. Lt. C. Howitt (Adj) Lt. J.Ripison O.O. Posted to A/152 RFA. D/152 Capt. A. Vernon-Taylor R.A.M.C. Reverted to Hospital Aug 31st Capt. Whyte A.V.C. " Aug 31st Interpret L'ABRE Capt. P.S. Myburgh in command of A/152 R.F.A. attached to 175th R.F.A. Lt. J.R.Budd " A/152 R.F.A. Lt. D. Wallis " A/152 R.F.A Lt. J. Fernie " A/152 R.F.A Lt. F.H. Lemin temp. attached to 36th D.A.C. 2/Lt B.W. Stirling " 36th D.A.C	
A/176				

INTELLIGENCE SUMMARY.

(Erase heading not required.)

1/76. F.F. Rate

Place	Date	Hour	Summary of Events and Information	Remarks and references to Appendices
B/176			Appendices	
			1. O'Callaghan posted to 14th Div.	
			Lt J.R. Sewell " B/160	
			" Nelson " D.A.C. 34th	
			" Bowman " A/160	
			" Pumphrey " DAC	
1/176			Capt G.T. Spain posted to C/160	
			Lt R Thorp " A/152	
			" T Payne " C/160	
			2nd Lt A.B. MacDonald " D.A.C. 34th	
			" W.H. Thomas " A/152	
			" Nichol " D.A.C. 34th

Lt Shape Lt RFA
Comdg 176 Bde RFA